U.S. CHEMICAL SAFETY AND HAZARD INVESTIGATION BOARD

I0502886

INVESTIGATION REPORT

VAPOR CLOUD DEFLAGRATION AND FIRE

(3 Killed, 4 Injured)

BLSR OPERATING, LTD.
ROSHARON, TEXAS
JANUARY 13, 2003

KEY ISSUES
RECOGNIZING FLAMMABILITY HAZARDS OF
EXPLORATION AND PRODUCTION
WASTE LIQUIDS
SAFE HANDLING OF FLAMMABLE LIQUIDS

REPORT NO. 2003-06-I-TX
SEPTEMBER 2003

Abstract

This investigation report examines a vapor cloud deflagration and fire that occurred on January 13, 2003, at BLSR Operating, Ltd., near Rosharon, Texas. The fire was caused by the release of hydrocarbon vapor during the unloading of basic sediment and water from two vacuum trucks into an open area collection pit. This report identifies the root and contributing causes of the incident. It makes recommendations on recognizing the flammability hazards of exploration and production waste liquids, and on safely handling flammable liquids.

The U.S. Chemical Safety and Hazard Investigation Board (CSB) is an independent Federal agency whose mission is to ensure the safety of workers, the public, and the environment by investigating and preventing chemical incidents. CSB is a scientific investigative organization; it is not an enforcement or regulatory body. Established by the Clean Air Act Amendments of 1990, CSB is responsible for determining the root and contributing causes of accidents, issuing safety recommendations, studying chemical safety issues, and evaluating the effectiveness of other government agencies involved in chemical safety.

No part of the conclusions, findings, or recommendations of CSB relating to any chemical incident may be admitted as evidence or used in any action or suit for damages arising out of any matter mentioned in an investigation report (see 42 U.S.C. § 7412 [r][6][G]). CSB makes public its actions and decisions through investigation reports, summary reports, safety bulletins, safety recommendations, case studies, incident digests, special technical publications, and statistical reviews. More information about CSB may be found at www.csb.gov.

Information about available publications may be obtained by contacting:
U.S. Chemical Safety and Hazard Investigation Board
Office of Prevention, Outreach, and Policy
2175 K Street NW, Suite 400
Washington, DC 20037-1848
(202) 261-7600

CSB publications may be purchased from:
National Technical Information Service
5285 Port Royal Road
Springfield, VA 22161-0002
(800) 553-NTIS or
(703) 487-4600
Email: info@ntis.fedworld.gov

For international orders, see:
www.ntis.gov/support/
cooperat.htm.

For this report, refer to NTIS number PB2004-100007.

Salus Populi Est Lex Suprema
People's Safety is the Highest Law

Contents

Contents (cont'd)

Figures and Tables

Figures

Figures and Tables (cont'd)

Tables

Acronyms and Abbreviations

AIT	Autoignition temperature
API	American Petroleum Institute
BLSR	BLSR Operating, Ltd.
BS&W	Basic sediment and water
CFR	Code of Federal Regulations
CSB	U.S. Chemical Safety and Hazard Investigation Board
DOT	U.S. Department of Transportation
E&P	Exploration and production
EMS	Emergency medical services
EPA	U.S. Environmental Protection Agency
°F	Degrees Fahrenheit
FM	Farm-to-market
FR	Federal Register
LFL	Lower flammability limit
MSDS	Material safety data sheet
mJ	MilliJoule
NFPA	National Fire Protection Association
NTTC	National Tank Truck Carriers, Inc.
OSHA	Occupational Safety and Health Administration
PVC	Polyvinyl chloride
RCRA	Resource Conservation and Recovery Act
RP	Recommended practice (API)
rpm	Revolutions per minute
RRC	Texas Railroad Commission
T&L	T&L Environmental Services, Inc.
TCLP	Toxicity characteristic leaching procedure
UFL	Upper flammability limit
VFD	Volunteer fire department

Executive Summary

On January 13, 2003, at approximately 4:30 pm, a vapor cloud deflagration and pool fire erupted at the BLSR Operating, Ltd. (BLSR), facility located 5 miles north of Rosharon, Texas. Two BLSR employees were killed, and three were seriously burned. Two T&L Environmental Services, Inc. (T&L), truck drivers, who had just delivered gas condensate storage tank basic sediment and water (BS&W) to BLSR, were seriously burned; one of these men died on March 2.

The fire was caused by the release of hydrocarbon vapor during the unloading of BS&W from two vacuum trucks into an open area collection pit. BS&W is an oil/gas exploration and production (E&P) waste liquid. The fire destroyed two 50-barrel (2,100-gallon) vacuum trucks and seriously damaged waste liquid offloading equipment and structures at BLSR. One of the vacuum truck diesel engines was the most likely source of ignition.

The oil and gas industry disposes of many thousands of barrels of E&P waste liquids annually, including potentially flammable BS&W. Although these liquids are exempt from Resource Conservation and Recovery Act hazardous waste management regulations, they are not exempt from hazard communication regulations of the Occupational Safety and Health Administration (OSHA) or hazardous material transportation regulations of the U.S. Department of Transportation (DOT). Furthermore, E&P waste liquids can have flammability characteristics that meet the definition of a flammable liquid in both OSHA and DOT regulations, thus posing a significant physical hazard to personnel.

The U.S. Chemical Safety and Hazard Investigation Board (CSB) found inconsistency within the industry in managing the potential flammability hazard of BS&W. In some cases, the flammability hazard is not identified or recognized, and work practices are inadequate for safe handling of the potentially flammable liquid.

The CSB incident investigation revealed the following root causes:

- Noble Energy, Inc., the shipper, failed to identify the flammability hazard of BS&W generated at its gas well production facility, and also failed to communicate the hazard to employees and contractors who were required to handle the flammable liquid.

On January 13, 2003 . . . a vapor cloud deflagration and pool fire erupted at the BLSR Operating facility . . .

The fire was caused by the release of hydrocarbon vapor during the unloading of BS&W from two vacuum trucks into an open area collection pit.

CSB found inconsistency within the industry in managing the potential flammability hazard of BS&W.

Noble Energy, the shipper, failed to identify the flammability hazard of BS&W generated at its gas well production facility . . .

T&L [Environmental Services] . . . did not require Noble Energy to provide vacuum truck drivers with a . . . document listing the potential flammability hazard of BS&W, nor did it identify the flammability hazard of the mixture in the vacuum truck tank.

BLSR . . . did not . . . implement safe handling practices when offloading flammable liquid . . .

- T&L management did not require Noble Energy to provide vacuum truck drivers with a material safety data sheet or other document listing the potential flammability hazard of BS&W, nor did it identify the flammability hazard of the mixture in the vacuum truck tank.

- BLSR management did not have effective hazard communication practices in place to recognize the potential flammability hazard of each shipment of BS&W, nor did it implement safe handling practices when offloading flammable liquid onto the mud disposal and washout pad area.

Contributing causes of the incident are summarized below:

- T&L employees did not understand the potential flammability hazard of BS&W in the product storage tank, nor did they understand that inadvertent mixing of hydrocarbon product with waste liquid when filling the vacuum truck tank most likely increased the flammability hazard of the truck contents.

- T&L and BLSR management did not implement safe work practices to minimize the generation of flammable vapor and to control ignition sources.

- Neither T&L nor BLSR management and employees recognized that the truck diesel engines presented multiple vapor ignition sources.

CSB makes recommendations to Noble Energy, Inc.; T&L Environmental Services, Inc.; BLSR Operating, Ltd.; U.S. Department of Transportation; Occupational Safety and Health Administration; Texas Railroad Commission; American Petroleum Institute; and National Tank Truck Carriers, Inc.

1.0 Introduction

1.1 Background

At approximately 4:30 pm on January 13, 2003, a vapor cloud deflagration[1] and pool fire[2] erupted at the BLSR Operating, Ltd. (BLSR), facility located in Brazoria County, Texas, 29 miles south of Houston and 5 miles north of Rosharon. Two vacuum trucks owned by T&L Environmental Services, Inc. (T&L), of Alvin, Texas, were unloading basic sediment and water (BS&W)[3] collected from two natural gas well sites owned by Noble Energy, Inc., Houston, Texas.

Two BLSR employees were killed, and three were seriously burned. One of the two T&L truck drivers who were seriously burned died on March 2. The fire destroyed two 50-barrel (2,100-gallon) vacuum cargo tank trucks owned and operated by T&L, and heavily damaged equipment and structures in and around the BLSR unloading pad.

The Rosharon Volunteer Fire Department (VFD) arrived on scene within 15 minutes of the 9-1-1 call. The Angleton VFD also responded. The fire was extinguished within 50 minutes. Two Life-Flight helicopters transported two of the burn victims to a local hospital. The other three victims were transported to hospitals by private vehicle or ambulance.

Because of the deaths and injuries caused by this incident, the U.S. Chemical Safety and Hazard Investigation Board (CSB) launched an investigation to determine the root and contributing causes, and to issue recommendations in an effort to prevent similar occurrences. The CSB investigation focused on:

- Determining the level of employer and worker awareness of flammable liquid hazards at oil/gas production wells and disposal facilities.

- Characterizing the flammability hazard of waste liquids to identify sources of flammable vapor.

- Identifying the potential ignition source.

---

[1] A deflagration is an ignition and rapid burning of an unconfined flammable vapor cloud at less than the speed of sound. Although it produces a pressure wave, the energy is less than that produced by a confined vapor cloud explosion.

[2] A pool fire is a flame over a puddle or pool of liquid fuel. The heat released by combustion of the vapor fuel supplies the energy to vaporize the liquid.

[3] The Texas Railroad Commission (RRC) defines "basic sediment and water" as a mixture of crude oil or condensate, water, and other substances that collects at the bottom of crude or condensate storage tanks.

1.2 Investigative Process

CSB investigators arrived at the site on the morning of January 15, 2003. Over the course of the investigation, they examined physical evidence; interviewed Noble Energy, T&L, and BLSR management and hourly employees; visited other oil and gas production wells in the area; interviewed oil/gas producers and trucking company personnel; collected and tested oil/gas well production liquids; and reviewed relevant documents.

1.3 Companies Involved

1.3.1 Noble Energy, Inc.

Noble Energy (formerly Samedan Oil Corporation) is a global oil and gas exploration and production (E&P) company founded in 1932. Average production in 2002 from wells located in eight states and the Gulf of Mexico was 327,451,000 cubic feet of gas per day and 18,110 barrels of oil per day, as reported on Noble Energy Form 10-K. Noble Energy is permitted by the Texas Railroad Commission (RRC) to operate oil and gas wells in Texas, including the CJ Waller and Roberts leases[4] in Brazoria County, the two well sites involved in this incident. The CJ Waller lease began gas production in spring 2002, and the Roberts lease began gas production in fall 2002. Noble Energy uses contractors to perform daily inspection and maintenance activities as well as to remove and transport condensate, oil, and waste liquids.

1.3.2 T&L Environmental Services, Inc.

Noble Energy contracts with T&L Lease Services, Inc., to provide various oilfield services, including transport of waste liquids from drilling and production wells to permitted waste disposal facilities. T&L Environmental Services (T&L), a subsidiary of T&L Lease

---

[4]A "lease" is a area that produces oil, gas, or oil and gas; or any group of contiguous wells producing oil, gas, or oil and gas of any number operated as a producing unit.

Services, is a Texas RRC-permitted oil and gas waste liquid hauler.[5] The company has been in operation since spring 2001 and employs about 15 personnel. T&L Lease Services subcontracted waste hauling to T&L Environmental Services.

Vacuum trucks and drivers are permitted and licensed in accordance with U.S. Department of Transportation (DOT) regulations. Figure 1 shows a typical 50-barrel vacuum truck, similar to the two that were destroyed in the January 13 incident. T&L management stated that the trucks were not authorized to transport flammable liquids; this was confirmed by truck tank manufacturing records (Section 5.4).

Figure 1. Typical vacuum truck used to haul oilfield waste liquids.

1.3.3   BLSR Operating, Ltd.

The BLSR facility is located 5 miles north of Rosharon, Texas, on FM521. BLSR employed 18 personnel. The facility has been in operation since the mid 1980s and is currently permitted by RRC[6] to operate five U.S. Environmental Protection Agency (EPA) Class II[7]

[5]The Texas RRC term "hauler" is the same as the DOT term "carrier." The hauler transports commodities on public highways in accordance with DOT regulations.
[6]Texas RRC Project #F14563, August 21, 1995.
[7]40 CFR 146.5(b).

waste liquid injection wells. It operates on a 24-hour/day, 7-day/week schedule.

1.4 BS&W Handling

1.4.1 Generation of BS&W

In gas well operation, the wellhead gas stream flows through separators to remove produced water and liquid hydrocarbons (condensate):

- The water is stored in an aboveground storage tank.

- The condensate is passed through a heater-treater that breaks down the hydrocarbon/water emulsion.

Condensate consists primarily of hydrocarbon liquid with trace amounts of contaminants, including water, paraffin, sand, and other materials. It is stored in aboveground storage tanks (Figure 2), where resident time provides further separation of the liquids and remaining entrained solids. BS&W settles to the bottom of the tank, and the lower specific gravity condensate floats on top.[8]

Condensate consists primarily of hydrocarbon liquid with trace amounts of contaminants, including water, paraffin, sand, and other materials.

BS&W settles to the bottom of the tank, and the lower specific gravity condensate floats on top.

Figure 2. CJ Waller lease water and condensate storage tanks.

---

[8]Specific gravity is the ratio of the density of a liquid compared to water. A lower specific gravity liquid (<1.0) is lighter than the equivalent volume of water and will float on top of water.

When the BS&W level in the storage tank exceeds a preset value, usually 8 to 10 inches, the Noble Energy contract gauger[9] notifies the waste hauler to remove it from the tank. The gauger verbally informs the waste hauler of the specific well site, tank(s), and volume of waste liquid to be removed. In accordance with DOT requirements, Noble Energy is responsible for identifying both the DOT hazard class of BS&W and the quantity of liquid to be transported,[10] in addition to complying with all other applicable hazardous materials regulations. The contract gauger may provide this information to the waste hauler.

Noble Energy is responsible for identifying both the DOT hazard class of BS&W and the quantity of liquid to be transported . . .

The waste hauler supplies the vacuum trucks and drivers to remove BS&W or other waste liquids from the storage tanks and to transport the material to approved E&P disposal sites.

1.4.2   Removal and Transport

The contract gauger informs the waste hauler of the quantity of liquid to be removed, stated in barrels of liquid or in inches of height in the storage tank.[11] The vacuum truck driver is then dispatched to the well site to remove and transport the waste liquid as follows:

- Identify the correct tank(s) and quantity of liquid to be removed.

- Insert a flexible hose through the top of the tank or connect it to the storage tank drain manifold (Figure 3), and then connect the hose to the vacuum truck tank inlet.

- Operate the vacuum pump and the appropriate valves until the specified quantity of liquid is removed from the storage tank.

- Close the valves, remove the liquid from the hose, and disconnect all hoses from the storage tank and vacuum truck tank.

Figure 3. Condensate tank drain manifold and valves.

---

[9]The gauger is a contractor to Noble Energy who is responsible for daily inspection of well site equipment, minor maintenance, adjustments, transferring fluids between tanks, and recording water and condensate levels in the storage tanks.

[10]DOT 49 CFR 173.22.

[11]The standard 12-foot-diameter storage tank holds 1.67 barrels (70.1 gallons) per inch of height.

. . . The ability to avoid condensate removal is dependent on the technique the driver uses to measure the storage tank contents.

Figure 4. Typical vacuum truck tank sight gauge.

. . . There is no accurate measurement of how much condensate is included in the BS&W loaded into the trucks.

The objective is to remove only BS&W from the bottom of the storage tank. It is important that the driver minimize the removal of condensate because:

- Condensate is an important source of revenue for the producer.

- Condensate is a flammable liquid; mixing it with BS&W may increase the flashpoint of the mixture to also meet the definition of a flammable liquid (Section 3.2.3).

All T&L drivers and other waste hauler drivers interviewed by CSB stated that they were clearly instructed to avoid removal of condensate when removing BS&W from the storage tanks. However, the ability to avoid condensate removal is dependent on the technique the driver uses to measure the storage tank contents. Some waste hauler drivers report that they use a gauge line[12] to "color cut"[13] the contents of the storage tank, providing an actual measurement of BS&W removed. Other drivers use the gauge line only to measure the total height of condensate plus BS&W in the storage tank before and after removal of the liquid. Some drivers use the sight gauge mounted on the truck tank (Figure 4) to estimate the amount of liquid removed from the storage tank.

The T&L driver prepares a service work order for the liquid transported. It includes the waste hauler's name, truck ID, driver's name, producer's name and well number, well lease name, truck size, date and time, description of work, total charges, and estimated quantity of liquid removed.

Other than information listed on the service work order provided with invoicing, T&L provides no records to Noble Energy that accurately document how much BS&W is actually removed from a tank, nor does the gauger measure or record BS&W height in the tank. The only record at the well site is through a subsequent tank level measurement by the gauger or condensate hauler. This can occur up to 1 day after BS&W is removed. The storage tank might

---

[12]Gauge line is a rope or chain weighted on the bottom and indexed in standard length increments (e.g., by foot). It is lowered into the storage tank to measure the height of liquid.

[13]Color cut is a procedure whereby a chemical is applied to the gauge line that changes color when it comes in contact with water, a significant constituent of BS&W.

continue to receive liquid from the producing well during and after removal of BS&W. Thus, there is no accurate measurement of how much condensate is included in the BS&W loaded into the trucks.[14]

1.5 BS&W Disposal

The BLSR disposal facility contains two waste liquid unloading stations—the saltwater disposal station and the mud disposal and washout pad (Figure 5). These stations are used to receive E&P waste liquids, including saltwater, freshwater, used drilling mud,[15] and BS&W.

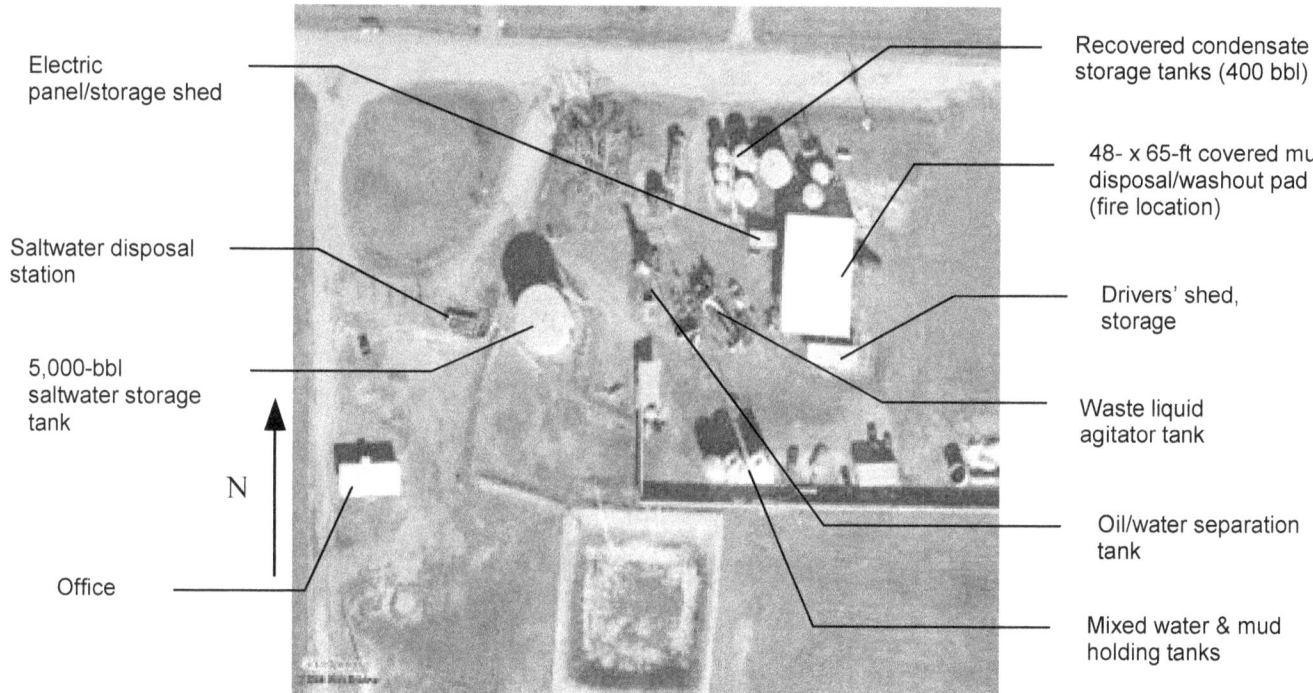

Electric panel/storage shed

Saltwater disposal station

5,000-bbl saltwater storage tank

N

Office

Recovered condensate storage tanks (400 bbl)

48- x 65-ft covered mud disposal/washout pad (fire location)

Drivers' shed, storage

Waste liquid agitator tank

Oil/water separation tank

Mixed water & mud holding tanks

Figure 5. BLSR facility layout.

---

[14]Noble Energy contracts with an oil hauler to remove and transport produced condensate/oil. The oil hauler prepares a "run ticket" or "refusal ticket" depending on the BS&W level in the bottom of the storage tank. In either case, the ticket accurately documents the BS&W level and the total liquid volume. However, this information is not routinely provided to the waste hauler for use when removing BS&W from the storage tank.

[15]Drilling mud is a fluid used to lubricate the drill string, line the walls of the well, flush cuttings to the surface, and create enough weight to prevent blowouts.

1.5.1 Saltwater Disposal Station

The BLSR disposal facility contains two waste liquid unloading stations— the saltwater disposal station and the mud disposal and washout pad.

The saltwater disposal station is used to unload "clean" salt and fresh produced water from oil and gas wells. Using a flexible hose connected to the vacuum truck and the truck-mounted vacuum pump, the driver transfers the truck contents to temporary holding tanks. Over time, the water, sand, and other solids debris entrained in the water sink to the bottom of the tank. Highly flammable condensate and crude oil, which might be present in the produced water, float on top. BLSR employees transfer this condensate/crude oil to the recovered condensate storage tanks. The condensate is sold to refineries; all remaining waste liquid is injected into the disposal wells.

1.5.2 Mud Disposal and Washout Pad

Although BS&W may contain significant amounts of recoverable condensate/crude oil (Section 3.1.2), it is typically unloaded at the mud disposal and washout pad. BLSR designed and built the mud disposal and washout pad for unloading high-viscosity drilling mud and other waste liquids heavily contaminated with sand and other materials, and for rinsing out empty vacuum truck tanks with high-pressure freshwater.

There are no provisions for recovering condensate/crude oil from the waste liquid that is unloaded onto the [mud disposal and washout] pad.

There are no provisions for recovering condensate/crude oil from the waste liquid that is unloaded onto the pad. It is injected into the disposal wells, as discussed below.

The 48- by 65-foot mud disposal pad is equipped with specialized pumps and other equipment capable of handling highly viscous and erosive waste liquids, including drilling mud, and paraffin and scale removed from pipelines. After the vacuum trucks are positioned on the pad, BLSR employees open the tank drain valves. Waste liquid splashes onto the large truck bumper (Figure 1) and then onto the pad. If the liquid does not adequately drain from the truck tank, the driver operates the truck-mounted vacuum pump. BLSR employees use high-pressure water hoses to dilute the high-viscosity materials, wash out the tanks, and wash the mud and other debris on the concrete pad to the sump area.

Two hydraulically operated lift pumps (Figure 6) transfer the waste liquids through polyvinyl chloride (PVC) pipes to an open-top waste liquid agitator tank located 40 feet west of the pad, or to the mixed water and mud holding tanks located about 70 feet south of the pad (Figure 5). Flexible hoses connect each pump to the PVC transfer pipes. Additionally, the pump discharge can be connected to a PVC header on the inside west wall of the pad to recirculate the liquid and further dilute the mud. Significant volumes of waste liquid, including potentially flammable BS&W, typically accumulate when offloading onto the concrete pad; the sump pumps have a lower flow capacity than multiple draining vacuum truck tanks.

The mud disposal and washout pad has a 3-degree slope, to a maximum depth of approximately 20 inches (Figure 7). A 12- by 12-inch wooden beam running the length of the pad, approximately 13

Significant volumes of waste liquid, including potentially flammable BS&W, typically accumulate when offloading onto the concrete pad . . .

Figure 6. Pad area hydraulic sump pumps and wooden stop beam.

feet from the back wall, protects the sump pumps by preventing trucks from backing too far onto the pad.

A corrugated roof canopy, approximately 17 feet high, covers the pad. Corrugated panels are also used along the north side of the pad to block the cold winter winds. High-pressure water hoses were suspended from the canopy for use in washing the truck tanks and in diluting high-viscosity mud both in the truck tank and on the pad area.

A 220-volt electrical service feed and circuit breaker box are attached to the southwest canopy support. Fluorescent lights attached to the canopy ceiling were used for nighttime operations. Droplights were suspended from the canopy. A large radial fan attached to the canopy was used as needed to vent noxious vapors during washing operations. With the exception of the droplights, none of the electrical conduits, fixtures, or boxes were certified for use in a flammable environment.

"No smoking" signs were posted around the pit area on the canopy support legs and on the nearby drivers' shed wall. An eyewash and chemical shower station is located 8 feet from the southeast corner of the pad.

With the exception of the droplights, none of the electrical conduits, fixtures, or boxes were certified for use in a flammable environment.

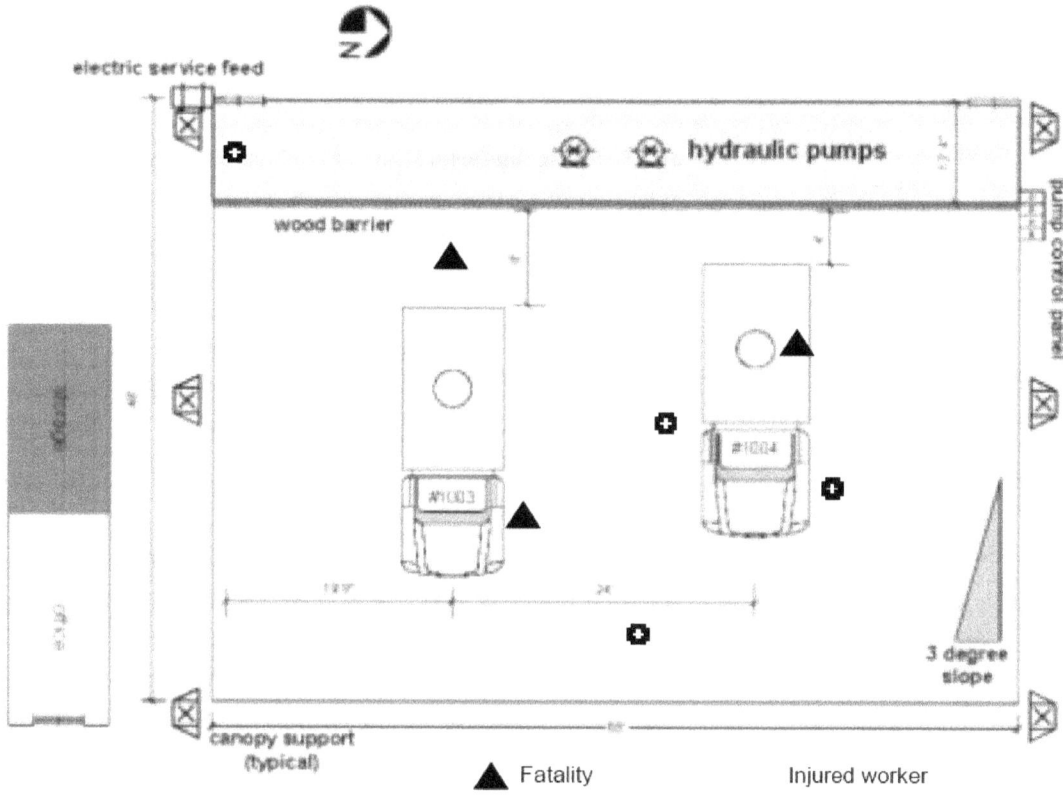

electric service feed

hydraulic pumps

wood barrier

pump control panel

3 degree slope

canopy support (typical)

▲ Fatality   Injured worker

Figure 7. Layout of mud disposal and washout pad,
with T&L vacuum trucks positioned as on January 13, 2003.

1.5.3   Other Facility Equipment

The BLSR facility included five water storage tanks and three storage
tanks for recovered condensate, which was periodically sold to oil
refiners. Injection well equipment included both electric motor
pumps and gas/diesel pumps for use during power outages.

The main office was located at the southwest corner of the facility,
about 100 yards from the pad area (Figure 5). A small office/store-
room—referred to as the drivers' shed—was located 8 feet south of
the pad. It was used by the truck drivers to prepare the BLSR
delivery slips and wait for their trucks to be drained or cleaned by
BLSR employees. The facility had a few additional utility sheds,
including the electric circuit breaker storage shed located 8 feet west
of the pad.

1.5.4 Operating Procedures and Worker Training

BLSR management had no written procedures for truck unloading, operation of systems, or emergency response. Employees learned their tasks exclusively through on-the-job training by BLSR management and experienced workers. Limited, general workplace hazard training was provided to some employees (using Spanish and English videotapes provided by the Texas Workers' Compensation Insurance Fund). With the exception of a summary of potential flammability hazards associated with waste liquids delivered to the facility, the employees received no other training on chemical hazards, nor were they provided with material safety data sheets (MSDS).

In terms of which unloading station to use, the only guidance provided by BLSR to the truck drivers was that "clean saltwater" was to be unloaded at the saltwater disposal station, and "dirty" water was to be unloaded at the mud disposal and washout pad. Drivers were also aware that drilling mud or other high-viscosity waste liquids could be unloaded only at the mud disposal and washout pad.

Attempting to unload such material at the saltwater disposal station could plug the piping and possibly damage the well injection pumps. BLSR provided only verbal instructions to explain which piping and valves were to be used at the saltwater disposal station.

In practice, BLSR relied on the truck drivers to decide which of the two unloading systems to use. Because all waste liquids—including clean saltwater and BS&W—could be easily and quickly unloaded at the mud disposal and washout pad rather than at the saltwater disposal station, drivers typically chose the former unless there was a backlog of trucks waiting to be unloaded. To avoid having to go to both areas, drivers also routinely used the mud disposal and washout pad to unload clean saltwater if the truck tank also required rinsing.

BLSR management had no written procedures for truck unloading, operation of systems, or emergency response.

In practice, BLSR relied on the truck drivers to decide which of the two unloading systems to use.

2.1 The Incident

At approximately 4:00 pm on January 13, 2003, the drivers of T&L trucks #1004 and #1003 collected BS&W from the CJ Waller and Roberts lease site condensate storage tanks, respectively. Both drivers relied only on the vacuum truck sight gauge to determine the volume of liquid removed from the storage tanks.

Oil hauler refusal tickets from the CJ Waller lease site recorded the BS&W level as 13 inches and 15 inches in two tanks—46 barrels total. The T&L driver reported 50 barrels of liquid removed from the tanks on the service work order. The records for the truck dispatched to the Roberts lease were destroyed in the fire.

The trucks arrived at BLSR within a few minutes of each other. Each driver backed onto the mud disposal and washout pad to unload BS&W and have the truck tanks rinsed out. The trucks were approximately 16 feet apart and equally distant from each side of the pad (Figure 7). Based on the service work order recovered from the drivers' shed and the vehicle license plate, the truck parked on the north side was #1004; the truck parked on the south side was #1003.

BLSR employees were in the process of diluting drilling mud that had accumulated from earlier deliveries by adding clean water and recirculating the liquid through the hydraulic pump and back into the pad area. Flexible hoses connected the pump to the PVC header mounted on the wall and from the header back onto the pad. Winds were from the west, at less than 5 miles per hour; the temperature was about 50°F.

The two drivers exited the trucks, left the engines running, informed BLSR employees that the trucks were to be drained and rinsed out, and made their way to the drivers' shed to complete paperwork and wait for the washout to be completed. Two BLSR employees opened the valves to drain the truck tanks. One BLSR employee climbed onto the truck parked on the north side of the pad and began to remove the manway cover bolts in preparation for the washout (Figure 8).

As reported by eyewitnesses, the trucks were in position for 3 to 5 minutes when the truck engine on the north side began to violently race/rev, slowed, and then violently raced again, blowing thick black smoke from the exhaust stack. A BLSR employee standing near the electric shed northwest of the canopy ran to the drivers' shed.

BLSR employees were in the process of diluting drilling mud that had accumulated from earlier deliveries by adding clean water and recirculating the liquid through the hydraulic pump . . .

Figure 8. North side truck manway bolts partially removed.

. . . The trucks were in position for 3 to 5 minutes when the truck engine on the north side began to violently race/rev, slowed, and then violently raced again, blowing thick black smoke from the exhaust stack.

BLSR employees and the driver of the north truck reported that they heard loud backfiring. The two drivers and a BLSR employee exited the shed and ran toward the trucks. The second (south) truck engine began the same violent racing. The BLSR employee proceeded to the area between the trucks, and each driver approached his respective side door.

At this point, a deflagration occurred. The BLSR employee standing between the trucks reported that the fiberglass hood on the south truck jumped up a few inches. Another BLSR employee stated that it looked like there was a flash of lightning under the south truck. The two trucks were completely engulfed by fire, as was the west end of the pit containing the liquid that had drained from the trucks.

2.2 Emergency Response

The BLSR owner and two employees in the main office heard what sounded like a muffled explosion and looked out the door toward the processing areas. They observed heavy black smoke at the concrete pad work area. One of them placed a call to 9-1-1 at 4:36 pm. Angleton Emergency Medical Services (EMS) and the Rosharon VFD arrived on scene at 4:50 pm. The Angleton VFD and Brazoria County Sheriff's Department were also dispatched. The firefighters reported an intense pool fire producing a large amount of thick black smoke and very intense heat, with flames 15 feet high. The fire was brought under control at 5:35 pm.

Two BLSR employees caught in the deflagration were fatally burned. The two T&L drivers were severely burned . . . one succumbed to his injuries 46 days after the incident.

Two BLSR employees caught in the deflagration were fatally burned. The two T&L drivers were severely burned and life-flighted to Herman Hospital; one succumbed to his injuries 46 days after the incident. Three BLSR employees sustained serious burns; two were transported to Fort Bend County Hospital by private vehicle, and the third was transported to Danbury Hospital by Angleton EMS. Two other BLSR employees standing near the pad were not injured.

The fire totally destroyed the two T&L trucks. Although none of the emergency responders opened the hood on the north truck during firefighting operations, debris from the hood was found in front of the truck, indicating that it was forced completely open by the deflagration pressure wave. The tank vent and drain valve packing and seals on both trucks were destroyed, as indicated by lack of resistance when moving the valve actuator handle.

The weight of the valve handle and internal components caused each of the drain valves to return to the closed position during the fire (Figure 9). However, even in the closed position, the fire-damaged valves allowed liquid to drain from the tanks. The sight glass was burned away, and the tanks were empty. All vacuum hoses were destroyed; only the coiled metal wire and connector fittings remained. Physical evidence also showed that the diesel fuel in the tanks did not spill to the pad area or contribute to the pool fire behind the trucks.

Figure 9. Truck tank drain valves
in closed position.

The canopy above the unloading pad sustained major heat damage (Figure 10). The electrical service line attached to the southwest canopy support column was severed, and all ceiling-mounted lighting and the vent fan were destroyed. The emergency eyewash station and shower next to the drivers' shed, the equipment switch panel on the northwest corner wall adjacent to the concrete pad, and equipment in the electrical shed sustained significant radiant heat damage. Fire and smoke damaged the storage room attached to the drivers' shed.

The fire department directed that the accumulated water and other liquid in the sump area be removed. A waste hauler transferred the liquid to two vacuum trucks and disposed of it at another licensed saltwater disposal well facility. Emergency responders completed their work at 10:00 pm.[16] There was no environmental damage.

Figure 10. Mud disposal and washout pad, showing burned trucks and damaged canopy.

---

[16]Brazoria County Sheriff Incident Report #03010143, January 22, 2003.

3.0 Incident Analysis

3.1 Hazard Recognition

Waste liquids generated at E&P sites include saltwater and freshwater, drilling mud, and BS&W—all of which can contain some flammable hydrocarbon liquids. The actual flammability hazard is dependent on the source of the liquid, ambient temperature, mixing during transfer to the vacuum truck, and other process variables.

Through interviews, CSB determined that many personnel in the E&P industry recognize the potential flammability hazard[17] associated with BS&W and other waste liquids, and implement safe work practices when handling and transporting these hazardous materials. However, more than two-thirds of those interviewed stated that they believe all BS&W possesses a negligible flammability hazard.

It is the responsibility of the offeror/shipper[18] to properly classify and describe materials (49 CFR 172, 173). However, CSB was unable to find any documents to support an analysis to determine the hazard class of the material being offered for transport by Noble Energy (e.g., MSDSs) or any other generator of the material. Haulers who are not notified by the shipper, or do not otherwise recognize the specific flammability hazard of BS&W, may fail to take the necessary precautions to prevent the occurrence of a hazardous materials incident. Furthermore, disposal facility personnel who incorrectly assume that BS&W is either nonflammable or presents a very low flammability hazard take few or no precautions to control flammable vapor generation and ignition sources.

The following Noble Energy, T&L, and BLSR management system failures contributed to this incident:

- Failure to recognize the potential flammability of BS&W, as defined by OSHA and DOT (Table 1), and to properly classify the material.

- Failure to implement work practices at the well site and at the waste disposal facility to minimize the release of flammable vapor from BS&W and to safely handle releases.

Waste liquids generated at E&P sites include saltwater and freshwater, drilling mud, and BS&W—all of which can contain some flammable hydrocarbon liquids.

. . . More than two-thirds of those interviewed stated that they believe all BS&W possesses a negligible flammability hazard.

---

[17] This recognition refers to an awareness that BS&W might ignite and burn. It does not imply knowledge of OSHA or DOT definitions of flammable liquids.

[18] The term "shipper" is the same as the term "offeror" used in the transportation industry.

- Failure to recognize potential ignition sources when handling BS&W.

- Failure to adequately train employees:

  - On techniques to minimize the potential hazards of flammable liquids.

  - On response to a system malfunction or site emergency.

  - On general awareness of and familiarization with hazardous materials.[19]

  - On specific job functions.[20]

Table 1

Flammable Liquid Flashpoints (a)

Flashpoint (°F)	Flammable Liquid
-100	Phillips Petroleum sweet condensate
-50	Unleaded gasoline
-40	Amerada Hess sweet condensate
30	CSB BS&W samples, CJ Waller and Roberts leases
45	Toluene
100	Diesel fuel

(a) OSHA 1A Flammable Liquid: Flashpoint below 73°F and boiling point below 100°F.

OSHA 1B Flammable Liquid: Flashpoint below 73°F and boiling point above 100°F.

OSHA IC Flammable Liquid: Flashpoint above 73°F and below 100°F.

DOT 3 Flammable Liquid: Flashpoint below 141°F.

---

[19]49 CFR 172.704(a)(1). Each hazmat employee shall be provided general awareness training designed to provide familiarity with the requirements of this subchapter, and to enable the employee to recognize and identify hazardous materials consistent with the hazard communication standards of this subchapter.

[20]49 CFR 172.704(a)(2)(i). Each hazmat employee shall be provided function-specific training concerning requirements of this subchapter, or exemptions issued under Subchapter B of this chapter, which are specifically applicable to the functions the employee performs.

3.1.1 Flammability Hazard of Production Liquids

Producers and haulers clearly recognize that producing well products—both oil and condensate—are flammable liquids. These liquid products are handled and transported according to Federal and state regulations. However, CSB found that the majority of those questioned during the investigation do not believe that BS&W exhibits a flammability hazard, even though it can originate from highly flammable condensate (Section 3.1.2).

OSHA does not require specific labeling of containers holding hazardous chemicals (e.g., flammable liquids) if the employer has an alternative method of communicating the hazard information. CSB observed that the labeling on well site storage tanks containing flammable liquids may not meet the OSHA standard. The tank ID number stenciled on the front of the storage tank may not be sufficient to adequately communicate the hazard to employees or contractors.

Of eight well sites visited after the incident, only three had labels identifying that the tank contained a flammable liquid. The other five sites had no markings on any of the storage tanks to communicate the hazardous material contents (Figure 11).[21] The only warning signs at these facilities consisted of "no smoking" signs attached to either the property fence or to the fence surrounding the storage tanks and associated equipment.

CSB concluded that labeling the storage tanks with the appropriate flammability hazard identification would not change the opinion of those in the industry who maintain that BS&W is not flammable—nor would labeling, by itself, have prevented the January 13 incident. However, labeling is likely to improve worker awareness and help ensure that less experienced individuals can distinguish tanks containing flammable condensate from tanks containing water.

Producers and haulers clearly recognize that producing well products—both oil and condensate— are flammable liquids.

. . . The majority of those questioned during the investigation do not believe that BS&W exhibits a flammability hazard, even though it can originate from highly flammable condensate.

Figure 11. Unlabeled flammable condensate storage tanks, CJ Waller lease.

---

[21]Following the January 13, 2003, incident at BLSR, Noble Energy attached labels to product and waste storage tanks at the CJ Waller and Roberts well sites, identifying the contents as DOT Class 3 flammable liquids. However, the product and waste storage tanks at three other Noble Energy well sites did not have any hazard class labeling on February 11, 29 days after the incident.

BLSR management reports that drivers have actually delivered condensate to the disposal facility when they thought they had collected water or BS&W from a well site storage tank; they had inadvertently removed saleable product liquid by drawing from the wrong tank. Proper storage tank labeling might help prevent future occurrences of this dangerous and wasteful practice.

CSB observed that the condensate storage tanks at two gas pipeline metering stations in the area, owned by a gas transmission pipeline company, were labeled with the National Fire Protection Association (NFPA) hazard diamond displaying a flammability rating of 4 (very volatile flammable liquid; Figure 12).

Figure 12. Condensate storage tank located at gas regulator station.

3.1.2 Flammability Hazard of Waste Liquids

Because BS&W and other waste liquids have a lower API gravity[22] (higher specific gravity) than condensate and oil, they gradually settle to the bottom of the storage tank. The measured flashpoint[23] of BS&W is dependent on the amount of volatile hydrocarbons contained in the mixture.

A higher temperature of the tank contents promotes separation of the hydrocarbons from BS&W. With the passage of time, more volatile hydrocarbons migrate up into the condensate, reducing the flammability of BS&W. However, there are no data to suggest a minimum residence time to separate sufficient volatile hydrocarbons from BS&W such that the flashpoint is increased above the hazardous flammable liquid threshold.

Production records for the CJ Waller and Roberts leases indicate that each well, in 48 to 72 hours, produces enough liquid to fill one 400-barrel tank. At this rate, it may be necessary to remove BS&W from the tank two to three times a week to maintain a satisfactory gas generation rate for the well. Establishing a minimum hold time to ensure that BS&W is no longer considered a flammable liquid before removal from the tank may not be a practical solution to reducing the hazard.

CSB analysis of nine tank BS&W samples from six production wells, including one of the wells involved in the BLSR incident, resulted in flashpoints below 30°F in eight of the samples. (For comparison, the flashpoint of condensate is about −36°F, and the flashpoint of gasoline is about −45°F.) Only one of the storage tank BS&W samples had a flashpoint above 141°F.[24] A tank bottom "thief" (Figure 13) was used to ensure that only BS&W was withdrawn from the tanks.

The measured flashpoint of BS&W is dependent on the amount of volatile hydrocarbons contained in the mixture.

Figure 13. Gauge hatch and tank "thief" showing 13 inches of BS&W below condensate.

---

[22] API gravity is a term used by the petroleum industry to express the relative quality, or heating value, of petroleum liquids. A high API gravity (low specific gravity) indicates a lighter crude with better heating value than a crude with low API gravity (high specific gravity).

[23] Flashpoint is defined as the minimum temperature at which a liquid releases sufficient vapor to form an ignitable mixture with air near the surface.

[24] The gauger measured 18 inches of water in the condensate tank. The water was deliberately put in the tank to add sufficient weight to prevent overturning by high storm winds.

Of the BS&W samples tested by CSB and Noble Energy, and those documented by EPA, more than 64 percent were determined to meet the DOT Class 3 flammability rating.

CSB determined that some BS&W—like condensate—may produce sufficient flammable vapors to pose an ignition hazard.

Tests commissioned by Noble Energy on BS&W samples from the CJ Waller and Roberts leases also resulted in flashpoints below 60°F and 30°F, respectively. In a 1992 EPA study of 32 production and reclaimer BS&W samples analyzed for flammability, 17 were found to meet the DOT Class 3 flammability criteria (USEPA, 2000; p. 26). Of the BS&W samples tested by CSB and Noble Energy, and those documented by EPA, more than 64 percent were determined to meet the DOT Class 3 flammability rating. Appendix A summarizes the test results. For comparison, Table 1 (shown on page 30) lists flashpoint values of selected flammable liquids.

As discussed earlier in Section 3.0, the E&P industry generally recognizes the significant flammability hazard of condensate liquids, but may not recognize the potential flammability hazard of BS&W and other waste liquids. CSB determined that some BS&W—like condensate—may produce sufficient flammable vapors to pose an ignition hazard. Inadequate recognition of potential flammability hazards results in inadequate hazard identification, inadequate hazard communication, and failure to safely handle and transport these materials.

3.2   Safe Handling of BS&W

Because the flashpoint of condensate is significantly below 141°F, it is a DOT Class 3 flammable liquid . . . It may also be classified as an OSHA Class IB flammable liquid . . .

Gas production well operations generate saleable condensate and liquid waste. The condensate is collected at production gas well sites and sold to refineries for use as feedstock. Because the flashpoint of condensate is significantly below 141°F, it is a DOT Class 3 flammable liquid[25] requiring special handling and transportation (Section 5.4). It may also be classified as an OSHA Class IB flammable liquid requiring specific equipment design to minimize the facility fire hazard (Section 5.3). E&P industry personnel, including haulers and disposal operators, understand the flammability hazard of condensate and handle it accordingly. The flammability characteristics of condensate are similar to gasoline.

---

[25] 49 CFR 173.120.

As discussed in Section 2.0, CSB determined that a flammable vapor cloud was ignited. There are two scenarios for the source of the flammable vapor—waste liquid offloaded in the disposal pad earlier in the day, or waste liquid delivered by one or both of the T&L vacuum trucks. Each scenario is discussed below.

3.2.1 Waste Liquid Deliveries Prior to Incident

CSB interviewed BLSR personnel who were working on the day of the incident. As summarized in Table 2, work ticket records identified 25 trucks (owned by 11 permitted waste liquid haulers) that used the BLSR facility between 12:00 am and 3:00 pm on January 13, before arrival of the T&L trucks involved in the incident.

The last truck, containing oil-based drilling mud,[26] was emptied on the pad and washed out approximately 2 hours before the T&L trucks arrived. BLSR employees reported that they had not completed diluting and washing the drilling mud into the sump pump

There are two scenarios for the source of the flammable vapor—waste liquid offloaded in the disposal pad earlier in the day, or waste liquid delivered by one or both of the T&L vacuum trucks.

Table 2

BLSR Delivery Summary for January 13, 2003

Work Description	Total Trucks
Empty tank washout	10
Deliver oil-based drilling mud and tank washout	2
Deliver dirty water	6
Deliver clean water	3
Deliver well fracturing waste liquid	1
Deliver well plugging returns	1
Deliver BS&W and tank washout	2

---

[26]Oil-based drilling mud is a specialized well drilling fluid containing mineral oil; it has a flashpoint in excess of 350°F and is not a flammable liquid.

intakes; a significant amount of mud remained on the concrete pad behind the wooden stop beam.

CSB determined from interviews that there was negligible drilling mud or other waste liquid above the stop beam prior to arrival of the T&L trucks. The concrete pad surface down to the stop beam had been thoroughly washed. Mud and other materials drained from the previous truck deliveries that day had accumulated behind the beam.

Furthermore, waste haulers familiar with BLSR operations confirmed that BLSR kept the concrete pad reasonably clean to preclude creating a slipping hazard for workers and truck drivers. The drilling mud and debris observed above the wooden stop beam after the incident were most likely forced past the beam by high-pressure water spray during firefighting.

There were two earlier BS&W deliveries on January 13 and two deliveries of drilling mud (which can contain trace amounts of hydrocarbons). However, area cleaning activities and the 2 hours between the previous truck delivery and the T&L vacuum truck arrivals would most likely have allowed any flammable vapor to dissipate. It is unlikely that the flammable vapor that ignited originated from the waste liquid remaining in the pad from the earlier deliveries.

. . . Area cleaning activities and the 2 hours between the previous truck delivery and the T&L vacuum truck arrivals would most likely have allowed any flammable vapor to dissipate.

3.2.2 Waste Liquid Delivered by T&L Trucks

CSB was unable to collect any sample of the liquid that was delivered to the BLSR facility in the T&L vacuum trucks on January 13. It was either consumed in the fire; or diluted with firewater, fire debris, and waste liquid from the mixed water and mud holding tank,[27] and removed from the scene during cleanup. Internal visual examination of the vacuum truck tanks 2 days after the incident showed both to be dry, with a negligible amount of residue. Either all of the liquid tank contents drained out before or during the fire, or the heat boiled any remaining liquid out of the tanks.

---

[27]The fire destroyed a PVC valve on the pipe connecting the mud disposal and washout pad to the mixed water and mud holding tank. The tank contents drained back into the pad area until a valve at the base of the tank was closed sometime during the firefighting activities.

One T&L shipping paper (service work order #105754) was recovered in the drivers' shed. It reported that T&L vacuum truck #1004 delivered 50 barrels of BS&W[28] from the CJ Waller lease. The remains of the truck on the north side of the pad were identified as truck #1004. Eyewitnesses at the CJ Waller lease confirmed that this truck picked up BS&W from the condensate tanks around the same time recorded on the work order.

The shipping paper for the second T&L truck, #1003, was not recovered. From interviews with Noble Energy well operations personnel, other T&L employees, and the Noble Energy gauger— and written records of condensate tank daily measurements—CSB determined that truck #1003 picked up BS&W from condensate tanks at the Roberts lease prior to arriving at BLSR.

CSB determined that the T&L trucks were in the process of offloading BS&W onto the concrete pad when the deflagration occurred. The flammable vapor that ignited most likely originated from this BS&W.

CSB determined that the T&L trucks were in the process of offloading BS&W onto the concrete pad when the deflagration occurred. The flammable vapor that ignited most likely originated from this BS&W.

3.2.3 Storage Tank Draining Procedures

The flammability of liquid in the waste hauler's vacuum truck tank is highly dependent on the procedure used to remove BS&W from the condensate storage tank and the physical characteristics of the tank contents. Figure 14 shows the position of the 4-inch-diameter condensate withdrawal nozzle and the 3-inch-diameter tank drain nozzle in relation to the bottom of a typical condensate tank. The flat-bottom, 12-foot-diameter tank has no internal piping.

If the total depth of BS&W drops below approximately 4 inches, condensate begins to flow out of the drain nozzle. If condensate is removed with BS&W, the hydrocarbon content of liquid in the vacuum truck tank is generally higher than the hydrocarbon content of BS&W. For example, if the BS&W depth starts at 10 inches (700 gallons, or 16.7 barrels) and the driver withdraws 8 inches of liquid

If condensate is removed with BS&W, the hydrocarbon content of liquid in the vacuum truck tank is generally higher than the hydrocarbon content of BS&W.

---

[28]Oil hauler refusal tickets recorded only about 20 barrels of BS&W in each of the two CJ Waller lease storage tanks (40 barrels total) 8 hours prior to the incident.

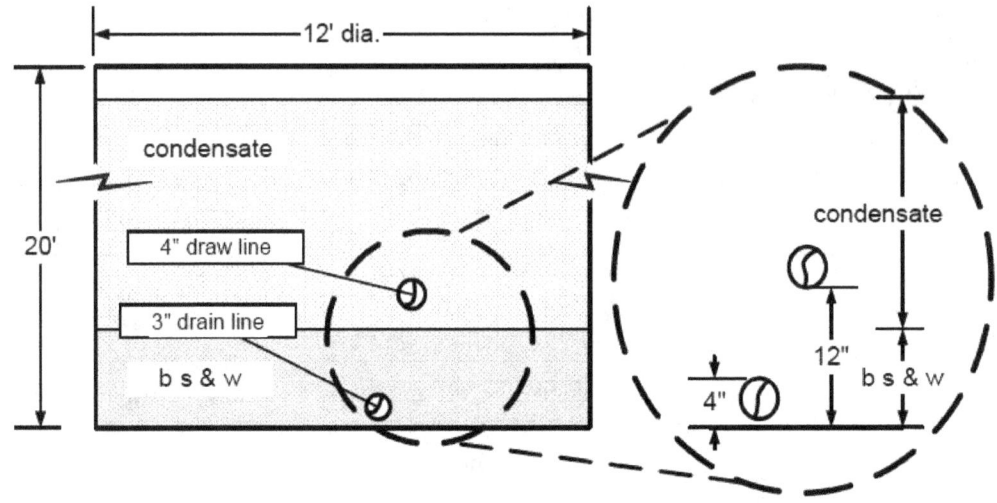

Figure 14. Vertical spacing of storage tank nozzles
(180° apart around circumference of tank).

(presumably BS&W) through the drain nozzle, as much as 2 inches of condensate (140 gallons) is mixed with BS&W. The liquid "waste" in the truck tank is actually 25 percent highly flammable condensate.

Some well operators require that vacuum truck drivers insert a hose through the gauge hatch on top of the tank to pull out BS&W rather than use the bottom drain, in the belief that this technique removes less condensate. However, pulling BS&W from the top draws condensate into the vacuum tank at least equal to the amount of condensate that fills the hose when it is inserted down to the bottom of the tank. Furthermore, this procedure requires close monitoring of the end of the hose to preclude it from moving up into the condensate during unloading. It also exposes the driver to additional work hazards, as noted below:

- Work must be performed on a platform at least 15 feet above the ground (Figures 2 and 11).

- Heavy hoses must be carried up the access stair, inserted into the storage tank, and tied to the catwalk railing.

- A hose leak could siphon flammable liquid out of the tank onto the ground.

Even if the "pure" BS&W in the bottom of the storage tank has a flashpoint above 141°F (a nonflammable liquid as defined by DOT[29]), the very narrow tolerance range involved with removal of BS&W increases the likelihood that the contents of the vacuum truck tank will have enough hydrocarbon liquid mixed in to lower the flashpoint below 141°F. The resulting mixture would then be classified as a DOT Class 3 flammable liquid, requiring special handling.

The viscosity of BS&W and the flow rate through the drain or suction hose also influence the amount of condensate that might be removed. BS&W with higher viscosity than the condensate or with a high flow rate causes a vortex effect (i.e., funneling) around the storage tank drain outlet or suction hose end. The liquid is drawn down much faster in the area near the removal point because there is insufficient time for horizontal flow to maintain the BS&W–condensate interface level across the entire tank diameter. This effect is further amplified because the drain and gauge hatch are located on, or very close to, the side of the tank—resulting in a much longer horizontal distance, typically up to 12 feet, for BS&W to flow to the removal port. Condensate is thus drawn into the removal port more quickly than when the flow rate is slow enough to maintain the interface level across the tank.

CSB determined that some waste haulers do not recognize the potential for removing significant quantities of flammable condensate along with BS&W. Control of this process is dependent on the measurement technique used by the driver, and the attentiveness of the driver in detecting condensate in the drain piping or vacuum truck tank, or in recognizing changes to the vacuum pump sound as condensate is drawn into the tank. However, even the best control procedure will not prevent condensate removal when BS&W drops below the top of the discharge port.

. . . The very narrow tolerance range involved with removal of BS&W increases the likelihood that the contents of the vacuum truck tank will have enough hydrocarbon liquid mixed in to lower the flashpoint below 141°F.

The viscosity of BS&W and the flow rate through the drain or suction hose also influence the amount of condensate that might be removed.

. . . Even the best control procedure will not prevent condensate removal when BS&W drops below the top of the discharge port.

---

[29]49 CFR 173.120.

3.3   Ignition Sources

As discussed below, there were five possible vapor cloud ignition sources—the vacuum truck diesel engine, vacuum truck electrical system, static electricity discharge from the offloading liquid, personnel smoking, and facility electrical wiring. CSB identified the diesel engine as the most likely ignition source, though high-temperature engine components and static electricity discharge cannot be ruled out. The other two possibilities were determined to be unlikely.

The vapor cloud could have been ignited by open flame or spark, or by a high-temperature surface. Each vacuum truck engine provided two possible ignition sources . . .

3.3.1   Vacuum Truck Diesel Engine

The vapor cloud could have been ignited by open flame or spark, or by a high-temperature surface. Each vacuum truck engine provided two possible ignition sources, as discussed in Sections 3.3.1.1 and 3.3.1.2.

3.3.1.1   Engine Malfunction Caused by Flammable Vapor

. . . If the intake draws a flammable vapor, the engine is likely to backfire through the intake system . . . Because the intake valve has not completely closed before ignition, the flame can travel back through the open valve and ignite the flammable vapor.

A possible source of ignition from the engine is a backfire through the intake or exhaust. Under normal operating conditions on a fuel-injected engine, there is no flammable vapor in the intake and exhaust systems. However, if the intake draws a flammable vapor, the engine is likely to backfire through the intake system.

A diesel engine relies on compression to ignite the air/fuel mixture. Backfire can occur if the addition of a flammable vapor sufficiently lowers the autoignition temperature (AIT)[30] of the mixture in the combustion chamber to cause it to ignite at a lower pressure (i.e., earlier in the compression stroke of the piston). Because the intake valve has not completely closed before ignition, the flame can travel back through the open valve and ignite the flammable vapor.

---

[30]AIT is the temperature at which a flammable vapor will ignite without an external source of ignition. AIT decreases with increasing pressure and increasing gas volume.

A second mechanism for diesel engine backfire is high engine speed such that the intake or exhaust valves cannot completely close before the air/fuel mixture ignites in the compression stroke. The valve spring rate determines the time required for the valves to close. If the piston speed (i.e., engine rpm) exceeds the limits of the valve closing time (a condition known as "valve float"), the air/fuel ignites before the valves return to the seated position. The flame propagates out of the combustion cylinder into the flammable vapor-rich intake or exhaust systems, the components of which can easily be blown apart. These systems are not designed for the positive pressures generated by flame ignition.

Blocking the flow of fuel to the combustion chamber by interrupting power to the fuel pump and injection system stops a typical diesel engine, like the ones in the T&L trucks. However, if a flammable vapor continues to be available through the air intake system, the engine will continue to run even when the fuel system is shut off. It is then necessary to block the intake or the exhaust gas flow to stop the engine.[31]

Some vehicle manufacturers include an emergency shutoff valve as standard equipment or an option. NFPA (1999) permits installation of a manual emergency shutdown device on the intake or exhaust systems to prevent engine overspeed. The U.S. Department of Labor, Mine Safety and Health Administration, and the U.S. Coast Guard require air intake shutoff devices in certain applications. Various Canadian provinces require diesel engine air intake shutoff devices on well drilling apparatus. However, preventing engine overspeed eliminates only one of the diesel engine ignition sources. High-temperature exhaust components may still ignite the flammable vapor, as discussed in Section 3.3.1.2.

A second mechanism for diesel engine backfire is high engine speed such that the intake or exhaust valves cannot completely close before the air/fuel mixture ignites in the compression stroke.

. . . If a flammable vapor continues to be available through the air intake system, the engine will continue to run even when the fuel system is shut off.

---

[31] Manual and automatic intake air shutoff devices are available to accomplish this function. However, these devices are intended only to prevent physical damage to the engine, not to prevent a backfire; they may increase the possibility of an accident if they inadvertently activate while the vehicle is moving.

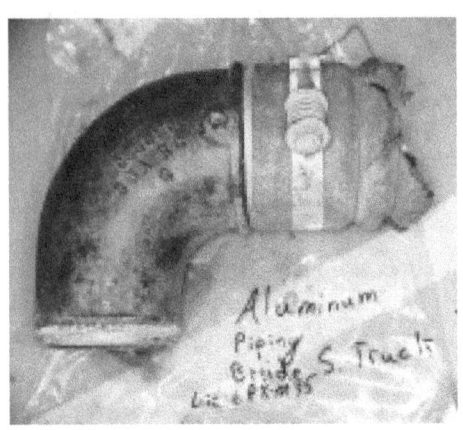

Figure 15. South truck diesel engine turbocharger discharge elbow.

The T&L truck engines were not equipped with overspeed protection devices in the intake or exhaust systems.

Examination of the truck engines and debris confirmed that the metal elbow on the south truck engine separated from the turbocharger housing— which is a positive indication that the engine backfired through the intake system, potentially igniting flammable vapor.

The T&L truck engines were not equipped with overspeed protection devices in the intake or exhaust systems. Eyewitness accounts of the over-revving are clear evidence that the air intake system was drawing in flammable vapor prior to the deflagration. Eyewitnesses reported hearing loud backfiring from one of the engines. Examination of the truck engines and debris confirmed that the metal elbow on the south truck engine (Figure 15) separated from the turbocharger housing—which is a positive indication that the engine backfired through the intake system, potentially igniting flammable vapor.

One witness also reported that the hood on the south truck lurched up just before the vapor ignited, suggesting a high-pressure impulse around the engine. The elbow and attached short piece of flexible hose (dark arrow in Figure 16) were recovered and showed no fire damage, providing further evidence that the fitting had come off and fallen to the ground before the fire ignited and destroyed the engine.[32]

Figure 16. Diesel engine exhaust and intake system.

---

[32]For comparison, evidence suggests that either the north truck engine did not backfire, or the pressure wave from a backfire was not sufficient to blow the fitting off the turbocharger. A portion of the elbow was still attached to the turbocharger housing, and the remainder of the elbow and flexible hose was destroyed.

In April 2003, a diesel engine maintenance shop disassembled the two truck engines to determine if either had incurred internal damage caused by over-revving, which would support the backfire scenario. The north truck engine sustained no damage indicative of overspeed. However, the south truck engine clearly showed evidence of over-speed damage, including a severely bent exhaust valve pushtube (Figure 17) and bent exhaust valve. CSB determined that backfiring from the south engine is the most likely source of ignition of the flammable vapor cloud.

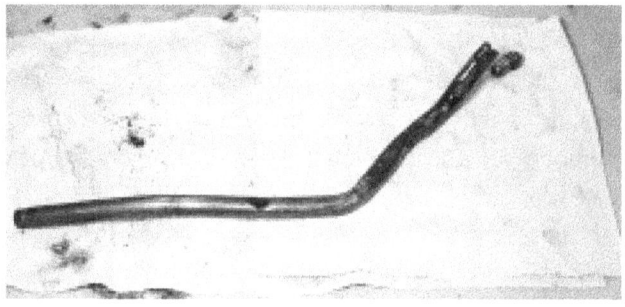

Figure 17. Bent exhaust valve pushtube, south truck diesel engine combustion chamber #2.

. . . The south truck engine clearly showed evidence of overspeed damage, including a severely bent exhaust valve pushtube and bent exhaust valve.

3.3.1.2 Surface Temperature

If a flammable vapor is within the lower (LFL) and upper flammability limits (UFL),[33] it most likely will ignite if it comes in contact with a hot surface at a temperature above the vapor AIT. Tests performed on BS&W samples removed from the CJ Waller lease and transported in one of the T&L trucks resulted in an AIT of about 560°F. For comparison, a condensate MSDS[34] identifies the AIT as 480°F.

A typical industrial diesel truck engine has many possible heat sources, including engine block and heads, and exhaust manifold and turbine housing (Figure 16). The engine block and heads are expected to

---

[33]LFL and UFL are the percent concentrations of a flammable vapor in air that will support combustion. Concentrations below the lower limit or above the upper limit will not ignite.

[34]Amerada Hess Corporation, Material Safety Data Sheet #15017, August 1998.

operate at about 200°F, near the boiling temperature of water. The exhaust manifold temperature is dependent on the engine load and cooling air provided by the radiator fan and truck speed. Thermal profile data provided by Cummins Engine show contact temperatures on the turbocharger mounting flange ranging from 270°F at idle to more than 1,000°F at full load.

CSB determined that the turbocharger flange surface temperature may have been hot enough to ignite the flammable vapor.

The T&L trucks had been driven at highway speeds from the well sites to BLSR, a distance of about 10 miles. When they arrived at the mud disposal and washout pad, they were directed into position and the unloading process began with minimal delay. CSB determined that the turbocharger flange surface temperature may have been hot enough to ignite the flammable vapor. Furthermore, vapor could have migrated to the turbocharger housing due to airflow from the engine radiator cooling fan. High temperatures on these engine exhaust components could have provided an ignition source for the flammable hydrocarbon vapor.

3.3.2 Vacuum Truck Electrical System

Sparks from the truck electrical system could ignite a flammable vapor if it is within the LFL–UFL range. Possible sources of electric sparks on the T&L trucks include damaged wiring, or electrical devices inside the truck cab or anywhere on the chassis. However, because of the total destruction of the trucks, it was not possible to identify any vehicle-mounted electrical circuits as a possible ignition source.

Possible sources of electric sparks on the T&L trucks include damaged wiring, or electrical devices inside the truck cab or anywhere on the chassis.

3.3.3 Static Electricity From Offloading Liquid

Hydrocarbon-based liquids are capable of accumulating a static charge as they flow through piping systems and hoses, or mix and slosh during transit. Water mixed in the liquid can exacerbate the static hazard. Only 0.2 to 0.3 milliJoule (mJ) of spark energy is needed to ignite vapor from hydrocarbon liquids; for comparison, static discharge from a human body to another object can exceed 0.4 mJ.

Proper grounding of equipment is critical to dissipating the static charge buildup to preclude a spark release. API recommends that trucks always be grounded when loading and unloading liquid, and also that conducting hoses be used to connect the truck to the equipment (API, 1999).

A retractable grounding cable was mounted on the rear bumper of the T&L vacuum trucks (Figure 18). However, there were no provisions at BLSR for attaching the truck cable to a suitable ground device. Hoses were not used during the offloading procedure.

Because the trucks were not grounded, unloading of the tank contents may have generated a static electric spark, which could have ignited the flammable vapor. Although this cannot be ruled out, the preponderance of evidence, as discussed in Section 3.3.1, suggests that backfiring caused by engine overspeed is the more likely source of ignition.

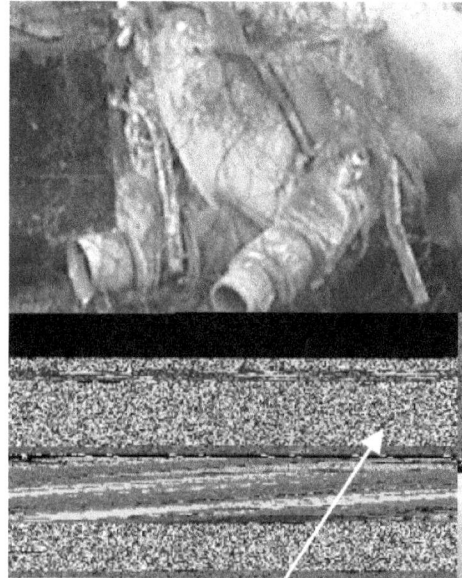

Figure 18. Truck-mounted ground cable recoil device.

3.3.4   Personnel Smoking

"No smoking" signs were prominently posted around the mud disposal and washout pad, and BLSR employees avoided smoking in the area. Eyewitnesses reported that neither driver was smoking when they arrived at BLSR or prior to the fire. Furthermore, no eyewitness accounts supported a scenario whereby smoking caused the vapor cloud to ignite.

. . . There were no provisions at BLSR for attaching the truck [ground] cable to a suitable ground device.

3.3.5   Facility Electrical Wiring

The following circuits were located in and around the mud disposal and washout pad (Section 1.5.2):

- Numerous 110-volt lighting circuits routed on the canopy and in the drivers' shed.

- A 110-volt circuit panel in the storage shed.

None of these circuits were designed for operation in a flammable vapor environment.

Figure 19. Remains of motor control switch panel.

Physical evidence and eyewitness testimony led CSB to conclude that the vapor cloud was not ignited by a facility electrical circuit.

- Motor control switches on the northwest corner of the canopy near ground level (Figure 19).

- A telephone in the drivers' shed, which was used immediately preceding the vapor cloud ignition.

None of these circuits were designed for operation in a flammable vapor environment.

The lighting in the canopy was used only at night. Switch positions found on the circuit breaker panel indicated that the lights were not on at the time of the incident, as supported by eyewitness testimony.

Radiant heat caused the majority of damage to the motor control switch panel, indicating that the vapor ignition did not originate from that location. Physical evidence and eyewitness testimony led CSB to conclude that the vapor cloud was not ignited by a facility electrical circuit.

4.0 Industry Associations

4.1 American Petroleum Institute

API provides detailed information on the safe operation of vacuum trucks and waste facilities, as noted below:

- API Order No. G00004, *Guidelines for Commercial Exploration and Production Waste Management Facilities* (2001), provides information on management, operations, and risk reduction at waste disposal facilities.

- API Recommended Practice 2219, *Safe Operation of Vacuum Trucks in Petroleum Service* (1999), provides information on common hazards and safe work practices and precautions for vacuum truck operations.

Both documents provide detailed guidance on the safe operation of equipment and facilities; however, neither addresses the increased hazards associated with unloading flammable liquids onto open areas. It is a much safer practice to contain flammable liquids in closed piping systems during transfer.

BLSR and T&L management were apparently not aware of this API guidance.

4.2 National Tank Truck Carriers, Inc.

NTTC is a trade association of approximately 180 trucking companies that specialize in the nationwide distribution of bulk liquids, industrial gases, and dry products in cargo tank motor vehicles. Its primary mission is to:

- Enhance the safety of the industry by providing relevant and useful information to carrier management.

- Exchange information with major shipper organizations to ensure safe, efficient, and cost-effective transportation policies.

NTTC estimates that more than 70 percent of tank trucks carry DOT-classified hazardous materials, requiring carrier management and drivers to possess special knowledge and skills, in addition to understanding and fully implementing all applicable Federal and state regulations.

T&L was not a member of NTTC.

5.0 Regulatory Analysis

5.1 U.S. Environmental Protection Agency

The Resource Conservation and Recovery Act (RCRA) of 1976 authorized EPA to regulate certain industrial wastes. RCRA Subtitle C contains the comprehensive regulatory program for hazardous waste management. In 1980, Congress specifically exempted from regulation under RCRA Subtitle C "drilling fluids, produced waters, and other wastes associated with the exploration, development, or production of crude oil or natural gas."[35]

In July 1988, EPA published a regulatory determination to continue the exemption of these oil and gas wastes.[36] It clarified the scope of the exemption to apply to "those wastes uniquely associated with primary field operations." In March 1993, EPA again refined the definition to address the applicability of the exemption to wastes generated by crude oil reclaimers and other processors, and storage and transporter activities.[37] It provided that:

- "Change-of-custody" (i.e., sale of goods from shipper to hauler or others) applies to product only, not to waste.

- Offsite transportation of exempt waste does not negate the exemption.

- Waste derived from treatment of exempt waste, including recovery of product, generally remains exempt.

- Vacuum truck rinse liquid is exempt provided that the truck contains only E&P exempt waste, and the water is not subject to RCRA Subtitle C.

The Texas RRC is responsible for oilfield waste materials management in Texas under a federally approved program.

In March 1993, EPA again refined the definition to address the applicability of the exemption to wastes generated by crude oil reclaimers and other processors, and storage and transporter activities.

5.2 Texas Railroad Commission

The State of Texas has more than 6,000 oilfield operators and 350,000 oil and gas wells; 76 inspectors monitor these activities (RRC, 2001). RRC regulates the petroleum industry, including oilfield production, oil haulers, waste haulers, and waste liquid injection facilities, as provided in the Texas Administrative Code,

---

[35]Solid Waste Disposal Act of 1980, Section 3001(b)(2)(A).
[36]53 FR 25446.
[37]58 FR 15284.

RRC is responsible for regulating oil and gas production waste management and disposal.

[The RRC] cargo manifest [regulation] does not require characterization of hazards. However, DOT requires hazard classification on shipping papers.

There are no RRC regulations on worker safety related to the flammability hazard of waste liquids or production fluids.

CSB concluded that neither the liquid waste hauler nor the disposal facility emphasized the importance of minimizing the inadvertent collection and disposal of crude oil or condensate when removing BS&W from production storage tanks.

Title 16, Chapter 3. The scope of these rules includes permitting of producers (shippers), haulers, and waste injection well operators; monitoring production quantities; and ensuring environmental safety (e.g., protecting groundwater). RRC also requires testing of production and disposal wells and associated equipment to prevent groundwater contamination.

RRC is responsible for regulating oil and gas production waste management and disposal. Sections 3.9 and 3.46 of the Administrative Code contain State rules applicable to EPA Class II injection wells. Hazardous oil and gas wastes are regulated by §3.98, "Standards for Management of Hazardous Oil and Gas Wastes." RRC does not regulate the transportation of material on public highways. Although it requires a cargo manifest under §3.72, it does not require characterization of hazards. However, DOT requires hazard classification on shipping papers (Section 5.4). At least one of the vacuum trucks was carrying the required RRC manifest; the fire most likely destroyed the second manifest.

RRC has authority to regulate resource conservation and safety under the Texas Natural Resources Codes, provided in Rule 85.042(b):

> When necessary, the commission shall make and enforce rules either general in their nature or applicable to particular fields for the prevention of actual waste of oil or operations in the field dangerous to life or property.

RRC has exercised its authority applicable to safety only in cases specifically related to hydrogen sulfide. There are no RRC regulations on worker safety related to the flammability hazard of waste liquids or production fluids.

CSB concluded that neither the liquid waste hauler nor the disposal facility emphasized the importance of minimizing the inadvertent collection and disposal of crude oil or condensate when removing BS&W from production storage tanks. RRC has not promulgated specific regulations on controlling the inadvertent removal and disposal of crude oil or condensate.

RRC has performed many routine inspections of environmental compliance and reporting requirements at BLSR, with no significant findings. On January 14, 2003, RRC inspected the facility because of the fatal incident on the previous day and issued no adverse findings.

OSHA has worker safety regulatory authority over oil production and waste disposal facilities, as specified in 29 CFR 1910.1200, Hazard Communication, which covers the identification of hazardous chemicals and communicating information about the hazards to all employees and other individuals who might handle the "chemical." Methods of communication include labeling and the use of MSDSs.

These OSHA regulations cover E&P waste liquids. Noble Energy did not communicate the flammability hazard of BS&W to employees or contractors handling this material at the well sites. The lack of proper hazard communication to the T&L drivers resulted in mishandling of the OSHA Class 1B flammable liquid and, ultimately, to release and ignition of the flammable vapor during offloading at BLSR.

In addition to worker right-to-know, confined space entry, and hot work, OSHA regulates workplace hazards involving the handling of flammable liquids. 29 CFR 1910.106(a)(19) defines "Class I flammable liquid" as any liquid having a flashpoint below 100°F, including mixtures where more than 1 percent of the components have a flashpoint below 100°F. None of the OSHA regulations are affected by the RCRA Subtitle C exemption of E&P waste liquids, as discussed in Section 5.1.

CSB commissioned flammability tests on BS&W samples from the two condensate tanks at the CJ Waller lease and from nine additional condensate tanks at six other lease wells. Ten of 11 BS&W samples met the OSHA Class I flammability criteria. The sample collection method used by CSB investigators ensured that the samples contained only BS&W, with no condensate. Noble Energy conducted flammability tests on BS&W samples from the two condensate tanks at the Roberts lease; those results concluded that BS&W was a Class I flammable liquid. Appendix A presents the flammability test data results.

OSHA regulations require that facilities handling Class I flammable liquids be designed to minimize the possibility of igniting flammable vapors. Requirements apply to special electrical equipment and spacing of equipment. BLSR did not apply these requirements to the design and construction of equipment exposed to Class I flammable liquids.

Noble Energy did not communicate the flammability hazard of BS&W to employees or contractors . . .
The lack of proper hazard communication to the T&L drivers resulted in mishandling of the OSHA Class 1B flammable liquid and, ultimately, to release and ignition of the flammable vapor during offloading . . .

OSHA regulations require that facilities handling Class I flammable liquids be designed to minimize the possibility of igniting flammable vapors.

The OSHA investigation conducted after the incident identified BLSR management system deficiencies, including the lack of an adequate hazard communication program and inadequate control of ignition sources.

The OSHA investigation conducted after the incident identified BLSR management system deficiencies, including the lack of an adequate hazard communication program and inadequate control of ignition sources. Prior to the incident, OSHA had never audited the facility.

5.4 U.S. Department of Transportation

With flashpoints below 141°F, oil and condensate are DOT Hazard Class 3 flammable liquids that must be transported in accordance with DOT regulations . . .

The lack of proper identification of the flammable liquid resulted in improper transport and mishandling at the waste facility, which directly contributed to release and ignition of the flammable vapor.

DOT has regulatory and enforcement authority for the transportation of hazardous material on public highways. Regulations cover the safe handling and operation of vehicles that transport hazardous material.

With flashpoints below 141°F, oil and condensate are DOT Hazard Class 3 flammable liquids that must be transported in accordance with DOT regulations for design, fabrication, maintenance, periodic testing, and labeling of bulk transport tanks (49 CFR 173, 177, and 178).[38] These regulations establish minimum training requirements for drivers, limits on work hours, and record-keeping requirements. As with OSHA, none of the DOT regulations are affected by the RCRA Subtitle C exemption of E&P waste liquids, as discussed in Section 5.1.

CSB determined that BS&W removed from the CJ Waller and Roberts leases and transported by the T&L vacuum trucks was a DOT Hazard Class 3 flammable liquid. T&L did not transport these waste liquids in accordance with DOT regulations. The shipping paper prepared by the driver did not describe the hazardous (flammable) material, nor did it list the hazard class, identification number, or packing group. In addition, the truck tanks did not conform to applicable DOT regulations. The lack of proper identification of the flammable liquid resulted in improper transport and mishandling at the waste facility, which directly contributed to release and ignition of the flammable vapor.

---

[38]These subchapters cover shipper and carrier responsibilities, such as proper classification and documenting of bulk transported materials, procedures for loading and unloading flammable liquids, and proper use of hazard placards to alert emergency responders in the event of a vehicle accident.

6.0   Root and Contributing Causes

1. Noble Energy management did not identify the potential flammability hazard of BS&W, properly class and describe the material, or inform employees and contractors of the hazard.

    ■ The required MSDS was not provided to the vacuum truck drivers.

    ■ Condensate storage tanks were not labeled with hazard information.

2. T&L management did not require the shipper to provide the vacuum truck drivers with an MSDS or other document listing the potential flammability hazard of BS&W prior to loading the truck, nor did it identify the flammability hazard of the mixture in the truck tank.

3. BLSR management did not have practices in place to recognize the potential flammability hazard of each delivered load of BS&W, nor did it implement safe handling practices when offloading flammable liquid onto the mud disposal and wash-out pad.

    ■ BLSR did not review shipping papers or conduct flammability tests to determine the flammability hazard of delivered waste liquids before offloading.

    ■ BLSR provided no means of grounding the vacuum truck on the waste disposal pad, an important safety precaution to reduce the possibility of static discharge.

    ■ BLSR unloading methods did not minimize or control the generation of flammable vapor during the offloading of BS&W; there was no effort to avoid uncontrolled splashing onto the open concrete pad.

6.2   Contributing Causes

1. T&L management did not recognize that the process of unloading BS&W from the storage tank is likely to increase its flammability due to the unavoidable removal of highly flammable condensate along with BS&W. Although management instructed drivers to avoid removing condensate, there was no written procedure.

2. T&L management did not implement safe work practices (such as those contained in API RP-2219, *Safe Operation of Vacuum Trucks in Petroleum Service*) to minimize the generation of flammable vapor and to control possible ignition sources when loading and unloading BS&W.

   - T&L treated all waste liquid as nonflammable, as reported by management and evidenced by the use of non-DOT certified vacuum truck tanks.

   - T&L did not inform the drivers that BS&W could present a significant flammability hazard, requiring special handling precautions, such as ensuring that the truck engine was upwind and far enough away to preclude contact with a flammable vapor source.

3. BLSR management did not use available industry guidelines (such as those contained in API Order No. G00004, *Guidelines for Commercial Exploration and Production Waste Management Facilities*) to establish procedures for properly identifying waste liquids and their associated flammability hazards.

   - BLSR relied on the vacuum truck driver to select the appropriate unloading system—saltwater disposal station, or mud disposal and washout pad—without consideration of the potential to generate significant flammable vapor and without adequate driver training on decision criteria.

   - BLSR did not provide appropriate training to employees or truck drivers on the specific hazards associated with unloading flammable liquids, methods to minimize generation of flammable vapor, and ignition sources.

4. T&L and BLSR management failed to train their employees on diesel engine overspeed as an indication of the presence of a highly flammable vapor.

   - The truck drivers and at least one of the BLSR employees responded to the diesel engine malfunction by moving closer to the trucks. If they had remained where they were or moved farther away, they would not have been injured by the fire.

   - There were no emergency procedures for safe and proper response to diesel engine overspeed.

7.0 Recommendations

Noble Energy, Inc.

1. Provide documentation of the potential flammability hazard of exploration and production (E&P) waste liquids—such as a material safety data sheet (MSDS)—to all employees, contract personnel, and haulers handling waste liquids generated at well sites. Emphasize that mixing condensate with basic sediment and water (BS&W) during the removal process can significantly increase the flammability hazard. The mixture in the transport container should be treated as a flammable liquid absent positive identification to the contrary. (2003-06-I-TX-R1)

2. Review and revise company gauging and waste liquid removal protocols as necessary to minimize the inadvertent removal and subsequent disposal of hydrocarbon product when removing BS&W from product storage tanks. (2003-06-I-TX-R2)

T&L Environmental Services, Inc.

1. Ensure that the written procedures for hazard identification require that all customers requesting loading and transportation of exploration and production (E&P) waste liquids provide written notification, such as a material safety data sheet (MSDS), listing the potential flammability hazard. (2003-06-I-TX-R3)

2. Ensure that the written procedures for safe operation of vacuum trucks incorporate applicable good practices, including techniques to minimize the possibility of exposing the diesel engine to flammable vapor, as provided in API RP-2219, *Guidelines for Commercial Exploration and Production Waste Management Facilities*. (2003-06-I-TX-R4)

3. Develop written operating procedures that incorporate best practices for unloading storage tank waste liquids, such that drivers accurately measure the quantity of liquid removed from the storage tank and minimize removal of product, such as flammable condensate. (2003-06-I-TX-R5)

4. Ensure that written emergency procedures address the safe response to abnormal diesel engine operation due to a flammable vapor atmosphere. Explain that the normal engine shutoff method will not function as long as flammable vapor continues to enter the intake system. (2003-06-I-TX-R6)

5. Conduct and document training for all personnel who handle waste liquids, using languages or formats that are clearly understood by all affected personnel. (2003-06-I-TX-R7)

  ■ Address the potential flammability hazard associated with E&P waste liquids, emphasizing how the withdrawal procedure is likely to increase the flammability of the vacuum truck contents through unavoidable mixing of product and basic sediment and water (BS&W).

  ■ Describe operating and emergency response to diesel engine overspeed caused by a flammable vapor atmosphere.

BLSR Operating, Ltd.

1. Develop a written Waste Acceptance Plan as recommended by API Order No. G00004, *Guidelines for Commercial Exploration and Production Waste Management Facilities.* (2003-06-I-TX-R8)

  ■ Require the shipper or carrier to properly classify the flammability hazard of exploration and production (E&P) waste liquids.

  ■ Require the hauler to provide information that identifies the flammability hazard of the material before accepting the load, such as a material safety data sheet (MSDS).

2. Develop and implement written procedures and provide training to employees on the safe handling of all waste liquids delivered to the facility in accordance with API Order No. G00004, *Guidelines for Commercial Exploration and Production Waste Management Facilities*; and API RP-2219, *Safe Operation of Vacuum Trucks in Petroleum Service.* (2003-06-I-TX-R9)

  ■ Include requirements for proper grounding of trucks and eliminating other sources of ignition (e.g., facility electrical equipment and smoking in unloading areas).

  ■ Ensure that the material is presented in languages or formats that are clearly understood by all affected personnel.

3. Develop written procedures and provide training to employees on unloading all flammable or potentially flammable E&P waste liquids. (2003-06-I-TX-R10)

   ■ Avoid unloading flammable liquids onto an open work area, such as the mud disposal and washout pad.

   ■ Include alternative unloading method(s), such as using a closed piping system to minimize vapor generation.

   ■ Ensure that the material is presented in languages or formats that are clearly understood by all affected personnel.

4. Develop written emergency procedures and provide training to employees on response to abnormal or emergency situations, including uncontrolled flammable vapor releases that can result in a fire or explosion hazard. Ensure that the material is presented in languages or formats that are clearly understood by all affected personnel. (2003-06-I-TX-R11)

U.S. Department of Transportation (DOT)

Publish an information document for exploration and production (E&P) industry employers (including producers/shippers/offerors, motor carriers, and disposal facility operators) involved in the transportation of basic sediment and water (BS&W) and other E&P waste liquids on public highways. (2003-06-I-TX-R12)

■ Emphasize the importance of, and responsibility for, properly classifying and identifying flammable waste liquids.

■ Reference the Occupational Safety and Health Administration (OSHA) requirements for obtaining material safety data sheets (MSDS) from the shipper and the required content of DOT shipping papers.

■ Include specific reference to this CSB Investigation Report and the American Petroleum Institute (API) recommended practices cited in this report.

Occupational Safety and Health Administration (OSHA)

Issue a Safety and Health Information Bulletin on the potential flammability hazard associated with bulk transportation of oilfield exploration and production (E&P) waste liquids.
(2003-06-I-TX-R13)

- Summarize OSHA requirements for proper hazard classification by the shipper and for the use of material safety data sheets (MSDS).

- Summarize U.S. Department of Transportation (DOT) requirements for proper hazard classification and manifesting of flammable liquids, approved container design, and periodic testing.

- Discuss safe handling to minimize the generation of flammable vapor and to control ignition sources from vehicle-mounted equipment and facility equipment.

- Discuss the need for the employer to provide all worker safety information in languages or formats that are clearly understood by all affected personnel.

- Summarize the requirements for proper labeling of storage tanks to clearly identify the hazard of the contents to all employees and contractors working at the well site.

Texas Railroad Commission (RRC)

1. Require that all permitted drillers and producers identify and document (e.g., material safety data sheet [MSDS]) the potential flammability hazard of exploration and production (E&P) waste liquids. Provide the information to workers and contractors in languages clearly understood by the recipients.
(2003-06-I-TX-R14)

2. Provide information (e.g., safety bulletin) to industry on the potential flammability hazard associated with basic sediment and water (BS&W) and other E&P waste liquids.
(2003-06-I-TX-R15)

   - Waste liquids can contain sufficient hydrocarbons to be classified as flammable liquids.

- The waste liquid removal method can result in removing significant quantities of flammable hydrocarbon product such that the mixture in the transport container may require classification as a flammable liquid under Occupational Safety and Health Administration (OSHA) or U.S. Department of Transportation (DOT) regulations.

American Petroleum Institute (API)

1. Revise API RP-2219, *Safe Operation of Vacuum Trucks in Petroleum Service*, and API Order No. G00004, *Guidelines for Commercial Exploration and Production Waste Management Facilities*, to discuss the hazards of unloading potentially flammable or flammable liquids onto an open unloading area, such as a concrete pad. Recommend other alternatives for minimizing vapor generation, such as unloading of flammable liquids into a closed piping system. (2003-06-I-TX-R16)

2. Communicate the findings and recommendations of this report to your membership. Emphasize that basic sediment and water (BS&W) removed from crude oil and condensate storage tanks requires special handling, in addition to compliance with Occupational Safety and Health Administration (OSHA) or U.S. Department of Transportation (DOT) regulations, if it contains sufficient hydrocarbons (either residual or mixed in during the removal process) to be classified a flammable liquid as defined by each regulation. (2003-06-I-TX-R17)

National Tank Truck Carriers, Inc.

Communicate the findings and recommendations of this report to your membership. Emphasize emergency response to diesel engine overspeed caused by exposure to flammable vapor atmospheres. (2003-06-I-TX-R18)

By the

U.S. Chemical Safety and Hazard Investigation Board

Carolyn W. Merritt
Chair

John S. Bresland
Member

Gerald V. Poje, Ph.D.
Member

Isadore Rosenthal, Ph.D.
Member

Andrea Kidd Taylor, Dr. P.H.
Member

September 17, 2003

8.0 References

Amerada Hess Corporation, 1998. *Sweet Natural Gas Condensate*, Material Safety Data Sheet #15017, August 1998.

American Petroleum Institute (API), 2001. *Guidelines for Commercial Exploration and Production Waste Management Facilities*, API Order No. G00004, March 2001.

API, 1999. *Safe Operation of Vacuum Trucks in Petroleum Service*, API RP-2219, March 1999.

Brazoria County, Texas, 2003. *Sheriff Incident Report #03010143*, January 22, 2003.

Chevron, 2001. *Unleaded Gasoline*, Material Safety Data Sheet #3205, November 28, 2001.

Exxon Company, USA, 1999. *Condensate*, Material Safety Data Sheet, Product Code 929335, March 22, 1999.

Lees, Frank P., 1996. *Loss Prevention in the Chemical Industry*, Butterworth-Heinemann, Vol. 1, Chapter 15.1.

National Fire Protection Association (NFPA), 1999. *Standard for Automotive Fire Apparatus*, NFPA 1901 A-8.2.4.1.

Phillips Petroleum Company, 1997. *Sweet Natural Gas Condensate*, Material Safety Data Sheet, CAS #68919-39-1, October 31, 1997.

Reible, Danny D., and K. T Valkaraj, 1999. *TCLP Characterization of Exploration and Production Wastes in Louisiana*, Louisiana State University, March 1999.

Texas Railroad Commission (RRC), 2001. *Waste Minimization in the Oil Field*, July 2001.

U.S. Army Corps of Engineers (USACE), 1998. *Engineering and Design: Removal of Underground Storage Tanks*, Chapter 12, Product Removal Procedures, EM 1110-1-4006, September 30, 1998.

U.S. Environmental Protection Agency (USEPA), 2000. *Crude Oil Tank Bottoms and Oily Debris*, January 2000.

APPENDIX A: BS&W Hazard Summary Table

Sample Name	Organization	Flammable Hazard		Comments
		Yes	No	
3-1	Noble (CSB)	X		CJ Waller Lease samples 1/17/03, DOT Class 3, OSHA Class IB
4-1	Noble (CSB)	X		CJ Waller Lease samples 1/16/03, DOT Class 3, OSHA Class IB
B6	Gury Petroleum (CSB)	X		Sample collected 2/11/03, DOT Class 3, OSHA Class IB
EPA-01	EPA, 2000	X		DOT Class 3
EPA-02	EPA, 2000	X		DOT Class 3
EPA-03	EPA, 2000	X		DOT Class 3
EPA-04	EPA, 2000	X		DOT Class 3
EPA-05	EPA, 2000	X		DOT Class 3
EPA-06	EPA, 2000	X		DOT Class 3
EPA-07	EPA, 2000	X		DOT Class 3
EPA-08	EPA, 2000	X		DOT Class 3
EPA-09	EPA, 2000	X		DOT Class 3
EPA-10	EPA, 2000	X		DOT Class 3
EPA-11	EPA, 2000	X		DOT Class 3
EPA-12	EPA, 2000	X		DOT Class 3
EPA-13	EPA, 2000	X		DOT Class 3
EPA-14	EPA, 2000	X		DOT Class 3
EPA-15	EPA, 2000	X		DOT Class 3
EPA-16	EPA, 2000	X		DOT Class 3
EPA-17	EPA, 2000	X		DOT Class 3
EPA-18	EPA, 2000		X	
EPA-19	EPA, 2000		X	
EPA-20	EPA, 2000		X	
EPA-21	EPA, 2000		X	
EPA-23	EPA, 2000		X	
EPA-22	EPA, 2000		X	

Sample Name	Organization	Flammable Hazard		Comments
		Yes	No	
EPA-24	EPA, 2000		X	
EPA-25	EPA, 2000		X	
EPA-26	EPA, 2000		X	
EPA-27	EPA, 2000		X	
EPA-28	EPA, 2000		X	
EPA-29	EPA, 2000		X	
EPA-30	EPA, 2000		X	
EPA-31	EPA, 2000		X	
EPA-32	EPA, 2000		X	
G3	Noble (CSB)	X		Sample collected 2/11/03, DOT Class 3, OSHA Class IB
G4	Noble (CSB)	X		Sample collected 2/11/03, DOT Class 3, OSHA Class IB
Roberts 250	Noble	X		Samples collected 1/15/03, DOT Class 3, OSHA Class IB
Roberts 251	Noble	X		Samples collected 1/15/03, DOT Class 3. OSHA Class IB
RW8	Noble (CSB)	X		Sample collected 2/11/03, DOT Class 3, OSHA Class IB
RW9	Noble (CSB)	X		Sample collected 2/11/03, DOT Class 3, OSHA Class IB
S4	Noble (CSB)	X		Sample collected, 2/11/03, DOT Class 3, OSHA Class IB
T1	Hillcorp Energy (CSB)	X		Oil well sample collected 2/11/03, DOT Class 3, OSHA Class IB
T1B	Hillcorp Energy (CSB)	X		Oil well sample collected 2/11/03, DOT Class 3, OSHA Class IB
W5	Noble (CSB)		X	Tank contained in excess of 18 inches water
TOTAL		29	16	

Subtree A

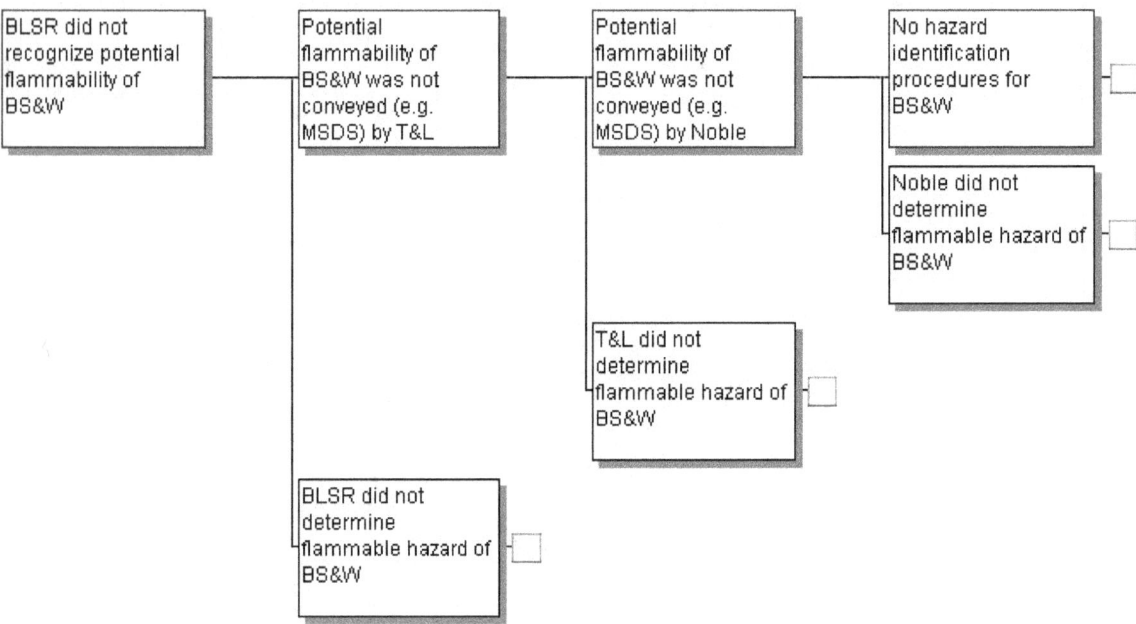

BLSR did not recognize potential flammability of BS&W

Potential flammability of BS&W was not conveyed (e.g. MSDS) by T&L

Potential flammability of BS&W was not conveyed (e.g. MSDS) by Noble

No hazard identification procedures for BS&W

Noble did not determine flammable hazard of BS&W

T&L did not determine flammable hazard of BS&W

BLSR did not determine flammable hazard of BS&W

www.ingramcontent.com/pod-product-compliance
Lightning Source LLC
Chambersburg PA
CBHW081607170526
45166CB00009B/2867